The Clever Teens'
Guide to
The Cold War

Felix Rhodes

Other works in the series:

The Clever Teens'
Guide to
The Cold
War

Table of Contents

War and Peace

From the end of the Second World War to the collapse of the Soviet Union in 1991 the world lived within the shadow of the Cold War. For almost half a century the East and the West eyed each other with suspicion and often hostility. Two ideologies, two political systems, two cultures, two superpowers fought for dominance, each firm in the belief that history would prove them right. And all the time the threat of a Third World War remained a distinct possibility, the spectre of nuclear weapons a constant fear.

War

During World War Two, the US and Great Britain were allies with Joseph Stalin's Soviet Union, united by a common goal – the defeat of Adolf Hitler's Germany and its allies. Yet, as soon as the guns fell silent, they were to become enemies in a 45-year conflict we remember as the Cold War. The heart of it lay in the capital of Germany, and the Berlin Wall, erected in 1961, became the most potent symbol of the Cold War years. Yet the extent of this East / West conflict stretched across Europe and across the globe as the US and the USSR continually sought for dominance.

It all started as a direct consequence of World War Two and the defeat of Nazi Germany.

On April 30, 1945, with Stalin's Red Army on the outskirts of Berlin and with the city reduced to rubble, Adolf Hitler took his own life. A week later, Germany surrendered. The war in Europe was over. Three months later, US president, Harry S Truman, authorized the use of atomic bombs on the Japanese cities of Hiroshima and Nagasaki. World War Two was over. It had cost some 60 million lives, two thirds of them civilians, destroyed cities and laid whole nations to waste.

Now came the torturous years of peace.

Peace

Germany lay in ruins, Great Britain was bankrupt and its

empire as good as finished while France licked its wounds after four years of Nazi occupation. A new world order emerged – two new superpowers, each as determined as the other to impose its will and principles upon the world. The Soviet Union (or the USSR) had suffered during the war – 25 million people dead, its agriculture and industry shattered; its territory devastated. From the smallest hamlet to the capital city, none had emerged unscathed and unscarred by war. The US, by contrast, had, strangely, benefited economically from the war. Although each individual loss is in itself a tragedy for someone, its losses, some 500,000 military deaths, were minuscule compared to the Soviet Union. Its civilians did not have their homes burned and their livelihoods destroyed. Yet, it emerged from the war full of insecurities. The vast expanse of oceans surrounding the country were no longer a guarantee of isolation and safety. The US needed to maintain its monopoly on the atomic bomb; and Europe had to be made safe, democratic and free in order to avoid a repeat of the turmoil that had allowed Nazi Germany to take hold during the turbulent years following the end of World War One.

Politically the two nations were very different. Russia was the heart of the working class revolution, home to communism. The US was, and still is, home to capitalism, democracy and freedom. But to Russia – capitalism was inherently unstable – didn't the US suffer from the Great Depression? And capitalism meant exploitation of the working classes and wealth for the oppressor, and the US was a nation that preached liberty but was full of racism and racial segregation.

British Prime Minister, Winston Churchill, US President, Franklin Roosevelt, and Soviet leader, Joseph Stalin, meeting at the Yalta Conference, February 1945.

During the latter stages of the war, US presidents, Franklin Roosevelt and, following his death, Harry Truman, met with Stalin and the British prime minister,

Winston Churchill, at a number of conferences. Here, united by a common foe, they agreed on how to defeat Germany and started discussing the make-up of a post-war world. Now, with Nazi Germany defeated, the uneasy and false wartime alliance fell away to reveal the degree of mutual hatred that had lain dormant while Hitler remained alive. It was each other they now viewed as the main threat to their security.

In the closing months of the war and the immediate post-war years, a number of countries found themselves torn between these two new superpowers.

Germany

The focus of this mutual distrust centred on defeated Germany and, at its heart, the destroyed city of Berlin within eastern Germany. Based on agreements made during the war, Germany and Berlin were to be divided into four sectors, each one administered by the four main allied powers – the US, Great Britain and France (in West Germany and West Berlin) and the Soviet Union (in East Germany and East Berlin).

Stalin wanted Germany punished. Understandable given the destruction his country had had to endure. He wanted the German economy shackled and demanded vast amounts of money (up to $10 billion) from Germany as compensation. But it was exactly this situation following World War One that had caused such poverty and misery, and had allowed Hitler and his Nazis to flourish. The US disagreed. Europe, the US felt, needed a strong Germany.

The 1940s

The Iron Curtain

In 1944, Stalin had promised to allow free elections throughout Eastern Europe. But he knew his communist parties stood no chance of winning these elections. In the national Hungarian elections of November 1945, the communists won a mere 17 per cent of the vote. But the Hungarian communists, as elsewhere in Eastern Europe (Poland, Romania and Czechoslovakia), bullied their way into positions of power. In March 1946, Churchill, no longer prime minister, delivered a speech in Missouri, in which he famously said, 'From Stettin in the Baltic to Trieste in the Adriatic, an iron curtain has descended across the continent'.

The Marshall Plan

In March 1947, President Truman declared the US's intention to 'support free people' throughout Europe. The president knew that the spread of communism had to controlled. He knew communism would appeal to people affected by poverty. From this came, three months later, the announcement of the Marshall Plan. Named after the man who came up with the idea, George C Marshall, Truman's secretary of state, the Marshal Plan would, it hoped, bring Europe back from the brink of collapse and contain Stalin's influence.

The European nations were invited to attend a conference scheduled for July 12 in Paris to discuss the plan. The invitation extended to the nations of Eastern Europe who, under strict instructions from Stalin, were not allowed to attend. Stalin saw George Marshal's plan as little more than the US's attempt to draw Europe under American and capitalist influence, and he remained determined not to let that influence extend to his area of control.

In the end, the Marshal Plan distributed huge amounts of money and agricultural and industrial equipment to countries in Western Europe. It helped the economic recovery following the ravages of war. Seventeen nations received aid which, by 1952, had reached the tune of $12 billion.

The Berlin Blockade

In June 1948, the Soviets cut off all road, rail and canal links between West Germany and West Berlin. The Berlin Blockade had begun. 'People of this world,' said the Mayor of West Berlin, 'look upon this city and see that you should not and cannot abandon this city and this people'. The communication channels of land and water may have been closed off but not by air. And so began the Berlin Airlift.

During the eleven months (318 days) of the Berlin Airlift, American and British planes supplied West Berlin with 1.5 million tons of supplies, a plane landing every three minutes, day and night. In the midst of this, ten nations of western Europe joined the US and Canada in forming a military alliance, the North Atlantic Treaty Organization (NATO).

On May 12, 1949, Stalin, knowing he couldn't sustain the situation indefinitely, stopped the blockade.

The Berlin Airlift: Berliners watching a US plane land at Berlin Tempelhof Airport, 1948.

Within two weeks, the political division of Germany became official when on May 23, 1949, West Germany was formally proclaimed in the city of Bonn. On October 7, 1949, came the proclamation of East Germany.

It was now formal – Germany was divided into two, East and West, and was to remain so for another forty years.

Thus, the 1940s ended with the two new superpowers having established their respective European empires, with Germany, now officially a divided nation, at its heart.

Israel

In 1948, the newly-formed United Nations decided to divide the nation of Palestine between the Arabs and the Jews, which meant the formation of a Jewish state. The Jews were as delighted at the prospect of their own homeland as much as the Arabs were appalled. On May 14, 1948, the State of Israel was formally declared. Immediately, this new nation came under attack from a group of Arab nations – Egypt, Lebanon, Syria, Iraq and Jordan. One million Jews from across the globe immigrated to Israel while 700,000 Arab Palestinians fled or were expelled. The Arabs were beaten back, and, following a nine-month conflict, Israel laid claim to having won what would be the first Arab-Israeli War.

China

Things were just as complicated in China. Before World War Two, China had been embroiled in a civil war between China's nationalist movement and its communists, led by Mao Zedong. With the outbreak of war, the nationalists and communists stopped fighting each other and agreed to join forces in order to defeat the Japanese invaders. With Japan's defeat in 1945, the civil war started again. Despite receiving American aid to the tune of $3 billion, the nationalists were eventually defeated. On October 1, 1949, Mao Zedong announced the formation of the People's Republic of China.

Mao Zedong proclaims the People's Republic of China, October 1, 1949.

The 1950s

Vietnam

In March 1945, during the war, Japan had seized much of French-ruled Indochina and now, in the post-war years, France wanted it back. Indochina comprised of modern-day Vietnam, Cambodia and Laos. During the Japanese occupation, the Japanese had ruled Vietnam through the long-standing emperor, Bao Dai. The Viet Minh, a nationalist communist group, fought against Japanese rule and then, immediately following Japan's defeat, declared Vietnamese independence, forcing Bao Dai to flee. The Viet Minh's leader, Ho Chi Minh, may have declared independence but power was still far from theirs – France was not letting go.

In 1949, France persuaded Bao Dai to return to

Vietnam in the hope that his presence would weaken support for Ho's communists. With the arrival of the former emperor, the Viet Minh immediately went on the attack. The communists won an important battle against the French in 1954. As a result, France agreed to withdraw its forces from all its colonies in French Indochina. Cambodia and Laos won their independence. Vietnam became temporarily divided at the half-way point in its country. The communists ruled the north, and Bao Dai in charge of the south. The UN announced that an election that would re-unify the country. In October 1955, however, Bao Dai was disposed. The new South Vietnamese leader, Ngo Dinh Diem, refused to allow elections. Vietnam remained spilt into two.

Korea

Like Vietnam, Korea was another country that found itself 'temporarily' divided into two.

During World War Two, the Americans and Soviets had decided that, following Japan's defeat, Korea should be divided north and south in the middle, and that they, between them, would administer the country. But neither the US nor the Soviet Union wanted any long-term commitment to the country, so the division was only designed to be a temporary measure until such a time free elections could determine who would run Korea as an independent nation. The communists, led by Kim Il-sung, took control of the northern half of Korea while in the south, Syngman Rhee, established his rule. Attempts at unifying Korea failed and in 1948 Korea officially became two nations: the Democratic People's Republic of Korea in the north, and the Republic of Korea in the south.

The Korean War: Korean children in front of a US tank.

On the June 25, 1950, North Korea, with Soviet and Chinese backing, invaded its southern neighbour. South

Korea, with the help of UN troops, fought back. Eventually, in July 1953, the two sides agreed a ceasefire. After three years of fighting and the deaths of some 1.2 million soldiers on all sides and 2.5 million civilian casualties, nothing had changed. The two Koreas remained intact, and the border remained fixed at the 38th parallel.

1953

1953 saw changes at the top. In January, Dwight D Eisenhower took office as US president, and on March 5, Joseph Stalin died following a stroke. He was replaced by Nikita Khrushchev.

Stalin's death promised, perhaps, a new era for those east of the Iron Curtain. That, at least, was the hope. But, as was soon to be proved in East Germany, nothing much changed.

On June 18, 1953, East German workers, fed up with their long hours of work and little pay, staged a revolt. The East German authorities, with Soviet backing, sent in the tanks. Many were killed. The East German protestors hoped for help from the West but the West was not willing to intervene and risk the situation turning into a war with the Soviet Union.

So, without the West's intervention, pockets of

resistance continued for a few weeks but the main thrust of the East German Uprising had been crushed within just 24 hours of starting.

On May 9, West Germany joined NATO. The USSR, alarmed by a NATO nation bordering Eastern Europe, immediately responded – on May 14, 1955, seven nations of Eastern Europe joined the USSR in establishing the Warsaw Pact as a counterbalance to NATO.

1956

On February 25, 1956, Khrushchev delivered a secret speech to his party leaders in which he criticized the recently-dead Joseph Stalin. The speech would become known as simply the 'Secret Speech'. But despite being a secret, the text of the speech soon spread across Russia and abroad. People were shocked that Khrushchev had had the courage to criticize his former boss but also relief that the Khrushchev may prove a nicer Soviet leader than Stalin.

Following Khrushchev's Secret Speech, the expectation of greater freedom from Soviet rule intensified. In June 1956 in Poznan, Poland, the workers rose up to demand economic reform. The Polish government responded by suppressing the revolt and killing some 100 civilians.

Demonstrations spread. The Poles managed to replace their hard-line leader with the more popular Wladyslaw Gomulka. Furious, Khrushchev flew to Warsaw for a showdown with the Poles. Gomulka, declaring his friendship, promised to remain loyal to the Soviet Union. Satisfied with this, Khrushchev returned to Moscow.

Following the success in Poland, Hungarian students and workers staged large anti-government and anti-Soviet demonstrations. They tore down a huge statue of Stalin in Budapest and demanded greater freedom, the right to worship, and protested against the excesses of the Hungarian secret police. Khrushchev ordered in the tanks but, hoping to improve things, replaced the hated Hungarian leader with the more popular Imre Nagy. With Nagy in place and the situation under control, Khrushchev withdrew his tanks – but only to the Hungarian border.

But then Nagy started promising free elections. This went too far for Khrushchev and he ordered the tanks back in. The demonstrators hoped for Western intervention – but it wasn't to be. Like East Germany three years before, Hungary was important but not important enough to risk a war. This time, the uprising was crushed and Nagy removed from power. (Two years later, Nagy was executed on the orders of the man appointed by Khrushchev to succeed him).

A child watching a Soviet tank in Budapest, Hungary, October 1956.

The Suez Crisis

Great Britain had been rulers of Egypt since 1882. In 1952, Egyptian army officers overthrew the Egyptian king, replaced him with a president, Gamal Nasser, and got rid of the British. In December 1955, the US, trying to please Nasser, offered to pay for the construction of a new, giant dam. But on realizing that Nasser was no friend of theirs, withdrew the offer. In return, Nasser, backed by the Soviets, took control of the Suez Canal in Egypt. The canal had been largely-owned by the British and the French since 1875 and remained vitally important to British interests in the area. In November 1956, British prime minister, Anthony Eden, believing that he had to show Nasser who was boss, launched an attack on Egypt. Khrushchev protested and threatened to retaliate. But, more surprisingly for Eden, he was heavily criticized by US president, Dwight Eisenhower. Under pressure from Eisenhower, Eden had to withdraw his troops. Britain's role as a major player in world politics effectively finished with the Suez Crisis.

The Arms Race

Following World War Two, the US had the monopoly on the atomic bomb. The USSR lagged behind. But with the help of spies working within the US atomic industry, as well as Soviet cleverness, the gap was soon closed. Truman upped the game by ordering work to begin on the hydrogen bomb (H-bomb), a thousand times more destructive than the atomic bombs dropped on Hiroshima and Nagasaki in August 1945. In October 1952, on the small Pacific island of Eniwetok, the Americans successfully tested the world's first H-bomb. Within a year, however, the Soviets had caught up. By the end of the decade, the US had raced ahead again and were developing intercontinental ballistic missiles (ICBMs) capable of striking the Soviet Union from American soil.

Khrushchev, determined not to be left behind, poured money into Russia's own experiments. Soon, they were experimenting with their own ICBMs. It wouldn't be long, warned Khrushchev, until the Soviet Union would be churning out ICBMs like 'sausages'. By the late sixties, both sides were developing anti-ballistic missile (ABM), missiles that could prevent ICBMs from reaching their target.

On October 4, 1957, the Soviet Union launched the first satellite, or Sputnik, into space. A month later, they launched the first living creature to orbit the earth – Laika the dog. The Soviets claimed Laika died painlessly in orbit about six days after take-off. We now know she died from overheating and in a state of panic within hours. Either way, shocked by how far the Soviets had advanced, the US stepped up their own space program. But the USSR continued to forge ahead – they were the first to reach the moon when, on September 14, 1959, an unmanned spacecraft landed on its surface. The US's first attempt at launching a satellite into orbit failed when on December 6, 1957, its rocket exploded on take-off. America felt it was fast becoming a 'second-rate power' in the Cold War behind the Soviet Union. In response, the US formed the National Aeronautics and Space Administration, NASA, and did finally succeed in launching its own rocket in

January 1958. But the ultimate humiliation for the US came on April 12, 1961, when the Soviet cosmonaut, Yuri Gagarin, became the first person in space in a round-the-world flight lasting 108 minutes. Khrushchev was delighted. President Kennedy responded by promising to have a man on the moon by the end of the decade.

Communist Witch-Hunts

The realization that communists working within the US were passing on vital and sensitive information to the Soviet Union caused a frenzy of alarm in the US. In February 1950, Republican Joseph McCarthy declared that he had in his hand a list of government employees known to be members of the American Communist Party. These informants, said McCarthy, were passing on information to the Soviet Union.

And so began the era of the communist witch-hunts.

McCarthy said there were communist spies working in Hollywood, America's universities, and the US army. People lived in fear of being accused of being a communist. In 1953 a young New York couple, the Rosenbergs, were executed for passing atomic secrets to the Soviets. The case intensified still further the paranoia of mid-50s America. McCarthyism was rampant.

Joseph McCarthy. Library of Congress.

Republican presidential candidate, Dwight Eisenhower, disliked McCarthy but needed his support to win the 1952 election.

In the end, the Republican Party had enough of McCarthy and in December 1954 stripped him of office, asking of McCarthy on live television: 'You have done enough. Have you no sense of decency, sir, at long last? Have you left no sense of decency?' McCarthy faded into obscurity.

China and the Soviet Union

China and the Soviet Union were the two largest communist powerhouses in the world. They were not, however, on easy terms. Nonetheless, Mao respected Stalin's position as the rightful leader of world communism. Following Stalin's death in 1953, Sino-Soviet relations began to sour. Mao considered Khrushchev weak and Khrushchev, although he extended the hand of friendship, never truly trusted the Chinese leader.

Mao began to stamp his authority in China. In 1958, he launched the ambitious 'Great Leap Forward' in order to modernize China. Mao wanted to modernize China's 'backward' agrarian economy and transform it, through rapid industrialization and collectivization, into a new, socialist society. In the countryside, 100 million peasants were forced into working on collective developments, such as huge irrigation projects. Mao demanded loyalty; he demanded 'More, faster, better, cheaper'. Projects were implemented too quickly, without enough planning. Those who resisted were severely punished. Those too old or poorly to be effective workers, were denied rations, and hence starved to death. The results were catastrophic – resulting in a devastating, far-reaching famine which, between 1958 and 1961, killed some 30 million civilians.

Sino-Soviet relations became increasingly frosty. Khrushchev's criticism of Stalin offended Mao. And Khrushchev's attempts at achieving a degree of friendship with the US angered the Chinese leader. Khrushchev, in turn, criticized Mao's Great Leap Forward and refused to help China develop its nuclear bomb. In the event, China had no need for Soviet aid – on October 16, 1964, China successfully tested their first bomb, becoming the fifth nation to do so – following the US, the Soviet Union, the UK and France.

The 1960s

Kennedy and Khrushchev

In the autumn of 1959, Khrushchev visited the US. The visit was deemed a success and helped ease Soviet-American tension. President Eisenhower and Khrushchev agreed to meet again in Paris the following year, this time with the leaders of France and Britain. They would discuss reducing the number of nuclear weapons. However, on May 1, 1960, 13 days before the meeting was due to start, the Soviets shot down an American U-2 spy plane flying over its air space in the Urals. Eisenhower denied any wrongdoing, claiming it was just a weather plane that had strayed off course. But the plane had crashed intact and the Soviets were able to produce evidence exposing Eisenhower's lies, not least the pilot, Gary Powers. The big meeting in Paris met on May 14. Khrushchev demanded an apology. Eisenhower refused, and Khrushchev stormed out.

Berlin

Kennedy and Khrushchev, June 1961. National Archives and Records Administration.

Berlin was not so much a source of strength for Khrushchev and Ulbricht, as a source of weakness. East Berlin was drab and poor compared to the glamorous, wealthy West Berlin, and East Berliners headed west. By 1962, the trickle of East Berliners heading to West Berlin had become a deluge – up to 4,000 a week, some 2.8 million East Berliners in all. Most of these defectors were the young; keen to provide their services and skills to somewhere where it would be better appreciated. On August 13, with Khrushchev's reluctant blessing, the East Germans erected a wall at the east-west Berlin border. The 12-foot-high Berlin Wall, the most potent symbol of the entire Cold War, was in place, and would remain so for 28 years. Kennedy was not happy to see the wall but, as he said, 'a wall is a hellova better than a war'.

Young child at the Berlin Wall, 1968.

Two years later, in June 1963, Kennedy visited West Berlin. In a famous speech in front of a crowd of 120,000 Berliners, Kennedy expressed US solidarity with the citizens of West Berlin and West Germany. 'Freedom has many difficulties and democracy is not perfect but we have never had to put up a wall to keep our people in ... All free men, wherever they may live, are citizens of Berlin, and therefore, as a free man, I take pride in the words, "*Ich bin ein Berliner*".'

The Cuban Missile Crisis

In January 1959, Cuban communist Fidel Castro disposed of Cuba's thirty-year-old dictatorship. Khrushchev was delighted.

The US, alarmed by the communist takeover in Cuba, decided to remove Castro from power. On April 17, 1961 a US-backed group of Castro-hating Cubans landed at the Bay of Pigs in Cuba, planning get rid of Castro. The invasion failed and over a thousand Cuban rebels were captured by Castro's forces. Kennedy was heavily criticized, while Castro enjoyed huge support.

Khrushchev decided to make use of this communist presence in the US's backyard. The US had a number of missiles in Turkey aimed straight at the Soviet Union. He decided to retaliate and place nuclear missiles in Cuba aimed squarely at the US. In Khrushchev's words, he wanted to give the US a 'little of their own medicine'. Castro gave his support and by the end of July 1962, the first Soviet ships had set sail for Cuba.

Photographs from an American U-2 spy-plane on October 14 exposed the missile sites and the presence on Cuba of medium-range Soviet missiles, well within the range of several US cities. Washington went into a panic.

Kennedy's speech on October 22, broadcast on radio and television, shocked the nation. The public clambered to stock up on foodstuffs and essentials, especially in cities listed by the American media as the most vulnerable to nuclear attack.

Kennedy's military advisors advocated direct intervention, but the president, not wanting to make the situation worse, instead implemented a naval blockade 500 miles from Cuba to prevent the arrival of further Soviet ships carrying missiles. But the US army and its nuclear weapons remained on red alert.

Eventually, the US and the Soviet Union thrashed out a deal. Khrushchev would order the withdrawal of Soviet missiles in Cuba in return for the withdrawal of the US missiles in Turkey, and, in addition, an American promise not to attempt an overthrow of Castro.

Two years later, on October 14, 1964, Nikita Khrushchev was forced from office. He was accused, among other things, of having brought 'the world to the brink of nuclear war' during the Cuban Missile Crisis. He was replaced by Leonid Brezhnev who was to remain the Soviet leader until his death in 1982.

The Soviets and the Americans continued their stockpiling of missiles. Both sides now had the ability to destroy the other. Yet by each possessing the means of annihilating the other, it strangely created a level of security – there was no point in destroying the other if it meant the other would destroy you. This strange logic was known as 'MAD' – Mutually-Assured Destruction.

Vietnam

Starting in 1961, Kennedy poured huge resources, money and men into South Vietnam, trying to prop-up the South Vietnamese leader, Ngo Dinh Diem. Diem, a strong Catholic, isolated and persecuted his Buddhist subjects, to the point Buddhists priests began demonstrating by setting themselves on fire. On November 1, 1963, Diem was disposed by generals of the South Vietnamese army. The following day he was assassinated. Three weeks later, in Dallas, John F Kennedy was also assassinated. His successor, Lyndon B Johnstone, continued and expanded America's commitment to defeating the communist north in Vietnam. The South Vietnamese army needed professional, US help.

In February 1965, the US declared war against North Vietnam. With public support behind him, Johnstone committed increasing amounts of military aid to the south, while Moscow and Beijing supported the North. From March 1965 to October 1968, the US subjected the north to continuous massive bombardment, Operation Rolling Thunder, but to limited political or military effect. The Vietnam War was a horrible experience for all those who took part. Inexperienced and nervous US soldiers killed innocent civilians. US forces used napalm to burn down forests, while US bombers incinerated whole villagers with napalm bombs. Chemical herbicides, nicknamed 'Agent Orange', poisoned crops and water.

The war was difficult but Johnstone felt he was slowly but surely gaining the upper hand. But on January 30, 1968, North Vietnam launched the 'Tet Offensive' against over 100 South Vietnamese cities and strongholds, managing even to hit the US embassy in Saigon. The US fought back hard but back in the US people were demonstrating against the war. The 'My Lai Massacre', March 16, 1968, didn't help. US soldiers killed some 500 villagers, including children, in this South Vietnamese village in the belief that it was a communist stronghold. The massacre, once exposed, shocked the nation, adding to the anti-war movement.

Anti-Vietnam War demonstrators, October 1967.

In January 1969, the new US president, Richard Nixon, took office determined to bring about 'peace with honour' and an end to the war in Vietnam. Instead, Nixon initially attempted to win the war through large-scale escalation, declaring, 'I will not be the first president of the United States to lose a war'.

In 1975, after almost 20 years of fighting, the Vietnam War came to an end. 58,000 US servicemen were killed during the Vietnam War, 250,000 South Vietnamese forces, 650,000 communist and up to 300,000 civilians. However, fighting between the north and the south continued for another year. The south were denied any further help from the US and in April 1975, South Vietnam collapsed. Saigon, the South Vietnamese capital, was renamed Ho Chi Minh City. Finally, on July 2, 1976, North and South Vietnam were merged to form the Socialist Republic of Vietnam.

China's Cultural Revolution

In May 1966, Chairman Mao launched the 'Great Proletariat Cultural Revolution'. Students and supporters of Mao formed themselves into 'Red Guards' and declared war on the 'four olds' – old customs, old culture, old habits and old ideas – and went on a nationwide rampage. Ancient buildings, churches, temples, cemeteries, libraries, archaeological treasures and priceless works of art were all destroyed in the name of communism and modernity. Believing in the 'justice' of their cause and loyalty to

Chairman Mao, the Red Guard recruits would be seen with a copy of Mao's book of quotations in their pocket. Mao's 'Little Red Book', as it became known, remains the second most printed book in history. Teachers, the educated, professional workers and even parents were attacked in an orgy of state-sponsored violence that rocked the country. In September 1967, with much of China in a state of anarchy, Mao, knowing he had to restore order, sent army troops to disarm and calm his Red Guard.

Czechoslovakia

In January 1968, the Czechoslovakian communist party appointed Alexander Dubcek as its new leader. Dubcek promised reform, democratisation and 'socialism with a human face'. He eased press censorship, allowed greater artistic and cultural freedom, eased travel restrictions, promised to guarantee civil rights and liberties and permitted a degree of democratic reform.

The Soviet leadership, under Leonid Brezhnev, became increasingly concerned with what they considered Dubcek's treachery and Czechoslovakia's counterrevolution.

In July 1968, Brezhnev, fearing Czechoslovakian independence, met with Dubcek and demanded that he reimpose strict communist control over his people and ordered Dubcek to reign in his 'counter-revolutionary' methods. Dubcek promised to do so but over the coming weeks it became clear to Moscow that nothing was being done.

Dubcek's failure to bring Czechoslovakia back in line angered the Soviet Union. On August 20, 1968, Brezhnev ordered in the tanks.

Half a million Soviet troops and 2,000 tanks moved in quickly, taking control of Prague's airport and vital points of communication before making a forceful presence on the streets of the capital. Dubcek was arrested at gun point, hit with a rifle butt and bundled into an aeroplane and taken to Moscow. In the Kremlin, Brezhnev, with tears in his eyes, shouted at Dubcek, 'I trusted you,' he said, 'you have let us all down'.

Dubcek and colleagues were forced into signing declarations of renewed loyalty to Moscow. He was returned to office in Prague, his work carefully looked over. Within the year, however, he was removed from power and exiled to a minor post. He was replaced by Gustav Husak, a man more loyal to Moscow and devoted to the socialist cause. Czechoslovakia's brief flirtation with reform and democracy, its 'Prague Spring', was over.

Husak immediately reversed Dubcek's reforms, rid the party of its more liberal members, and imposed greater authoritarian control over the country, a process referred to as 'normalization'. (Husak was to remain in power until the collapse of Czechoslovakia in December 1989.)

There were minor protests against the re-imposition of authoritarian rule, most notably on January 16, 1969 when a student, Jan Palach, set himself on fire in Prague's Wenceslas Square. Palach was to die of his injuries three days later.

The 1960s finished with one of the defining moments of the twentieth century – the first man on the moon. US astronaut, Neil Armstrong, claimed his place in history by stepping on the moon's surface on July 21, 1969. Kennedy's promise, eight years earlier, that the US would put a man on the moon before the end of the decade had come true.

The 1970s

Détente

The new American president, Richard Nixon, was determined to improve US-Soviet relations. Indeed, relations between the two superpowers had eased since the Cuban Missile Crisis, entering a period known as 'détente'. Meanwhile, relations between the communist heavyweights, Soviet Union and China, which had deteriorated following Stalin's death in 1953, took a turn for the worse. Sino-Soviet border clashes broke out in 1969 and for a while escalation was a serious possibility.

On May 26, 1972 Nixon and Brezhnev signed an agreement, limiting the production of nuclear weapons. Both sides agreed to settle their differences by 'peaceful means'. Nixon's appearance in Moscow in May 1972, the first US president to visit the Soviet Union since World War Two, was, in itself, a significant step in the spirit of détente. Three months earlier, February 1972, Nixon had also visited Chairman Mao in Beijing.

Mao and Nixon, 29 February 1972. Richard Nixon Presidential Library and Museum.

But Richard Nixon was not to survive as president for much longer. A national scandal involving Nixon and a break-in on June 17, 1972 at the Democratic headquarters at the Watergate complex in Washington, D.C. rocked the nation. Nixon's attempts to lie failed. On August 9, 1974, Nixon resigned, the first and only US president to resign from presidential office.

The Yom Kippur War

In 1973, conflict in the Middle East flared up again. Egypt's president, Gamal Nasser, had died in 1970. He had been replaced by Anwar Sadat. Under Sadat's control, Egypt and a coalition of Arab states attacked Israel on October 6, 1973, the Jewish festival day of Yom Kippur. His aim – to recapture territory lost to Israel during a previous war which had taken place in 1967. Initial Arab advances were soon beaten back. The Soviets and the US shouted from the sidelines, supporting and supplying Egypt and Israel respectively. Urgent and frantic talks were held but tensions rose. On October 25, Nixon put the US on high nuclear alert. The war had escalated into the worse US-Soviet confrontation since the Cuban Missile Crisis eleven years earlier. Finally, a ceasefire was agreed – but at a high cost... détente was as good as dead. Despite their pledges to work together, the Yom Kippur War had illustrated the gulf that still existed between the superpowers.

Iran

Mohammad Reza Shah Pahlavi had ruled as Shah of Iran since 1941. The shah ruled with an iron fist and made good use of his secret police, but, more importantly for the US, he was pro-American. Traditional Muslims followed the Shi'ite leader, the Ayatollah Khomeini. In the 1960s, the Ayatollah began writing and preaching against the Shah, accusing him of promoting 'Western decadence' at the cost of Islam. On December 11, 1978, a massive demonstration in Tehran, capital of Iran, called for Khomeini to lead Iran in a revolution and overthrow the Shah. Terrified, the Shah made last-minute efforts to form a new democratic government and dismantle his secret police in the hope of restoring his subjects' faith in him. It was too late. The crowds, ignoring these efforts, still called for Khomeini's return from exile. Admitting defeat, the Shah left Iran forever on January 16, 1979.

Khomeini landed in Tehran on February 1, 1979 to formally lead the Iranian revolution. Declared February 11, Iran was now an Islamic republic.

Meanwhile, the former Shah was granted asylum in the US. On November 4, a group of Khomeini's followers stormed the US embassy in Tehran and seized its staff. 52 American diplomats and citizens were taken hostage. The hostage-takers demanded that the US return the former shah to Iran to face charges. President Carter refused. Carter's attempt to rescue the hostages on April 24, 1980 failed – a humiliation for the US and, in election year, for Carter himself. Finally, after 444 days of captivity, the hostages were released on January 20, 1981 – the same day as Ronald Reagan was sworn in as the new US president.

The 1980s

Afghanistan

In the late 1970s, the Soviet Union, fearing that Afghanistan was falling from its influence, decided to act. On December 24, 1979, Soviet forces seized the presidential palace, killing the Afghan president, and installing a puppet regime with Babrak Karmal in charge.

The US protested loudly against the Soviet invasion of Afghanistan, and immediately imposed a grain embargo against the Soviet Union and drastically increased military spending. US missiles were installed in Western Europe, resulting in huge peace demonstrations.

Poland

On October 16, 1978, Cardinal Karol Wojtyla was appointed Pope John Paul II, Poland's first pope and the first non-Italian pope for almost 500 years. The effect on the citizens of Poland, caught behind the Iron Curtain, was immediate – they began to hope. Pope John Paul's visit to Poland drew millions to the streets. Speaking to a huge crowd in Warsaw on June 2, 1979, he declared, 'Christ cannot be kept out of the history of man in any part of the globe. The exclusion of Christ from the history of man is an act against man'.

Political unrest followed. In August 1980, dockworkers in Gdansk went on strike. One striker in particular emerged as their spokesman and leader – Lech Walesa. Initially, the strikers demanded economic reforms but soon they called for much more – freedom of speech, freedom of worship, and much more. They formed a trade union, Solidarity, the first independent trade union in the Eastern Bloc, with Walesa its leader. Reluctantly, the communist government in Poland recognised Solidarity – political prisoners were freed, the laws of censorship and religious worship relaxed.

Moscow, far from happy at this turn of events in Poland, urged the communist government in Poland to take a tougher line. They did. On December 13, 1981, the Polish government imposed martial law. Thousands of Solidarity members were arrested and imprisoned. Walesa himself was jailed for 11 months; a year later he was awarded the Nobel Peace Prize. Solidarity was outlawed in October 1982. Martial law was finally lifted in July 1983. But it didn't stop the intimidation, and arrests continued.

Martial law in Poland, 1981.

On March 8, 1983, US president, Ronald Reagan, called the USSR an 'evil empire' and criticized the lack of free elections in Eastern Europe: He announced the development of laser weapons which would, once employed, be capable of destroying incoming missiles whilst leaving America's own offensive missiles free to

45

reach their targets. So although labelled 'defensive', the Soviet Union regarded SDIs as an offensive development because, in effect, Star Wars destroyed the balance of Mutually-Assured Destruction that had kept the superpowers in check for over thirty years.

US – USSR relations, already at the lowest ebb since 1962, plummeted further when, on September 1, 1983, Soviet aircraft shot down a Korean civilian airliner over the Sea of Japan. All 269 passengers and crew aboard were killed, including 63 Americans and a US congressman. At first, the Soviets denied all responsibility, claiming they mistook the plane for a spy plane.

Gorbachev

Leonid Brezhnev died aged 75 in 1982. He was succeeded by the 68-year-old former KGB chief, Yuri Andropov. Andropov died on February 9, 1984 after only 15 months in office, to be succeeded by the 73-year old Konstantin Chernenko, who was already terminally ill. Chernenko had 13 months in office, dying on March 10, 1985. Reagan joked how could he meet with the Russians if 'they keep dying on me?' (Although Reagan himself was seven months older than Chernenko). Finally, a 'youngster' took over, the 54-year-old Mikhail Gorbachev, the youngest leader in Soviet history.

Gorbachev was a very different man to his predecessors. He knew the Soviet Union could no longer keep pace with the US's military arsenal and trying to do so was crippling the Soviet economy. He met Reagan for the first time in Geneva in November 1985. 'The United States and the Soviet Union are the two greatest countries on Earth, the superpowers,' said Reagan. 'They are the only ones who can start World War Three, but also the only two countries that could bring peace to the world.'

Reagan and Gorbachev meeting at the Geneva Summit in Switzerland, November 1985.

In June 1987 Reagan visited Berlin and, like Kennedy a quarter of a century before, inspected the Berlin Wall. 'Mr Gorbachev,' he demanded in a televised speech, 'tear down this wall!'

The Soviet public had been kept in the dark regarding the human and financial cost of their nation's commitment in Afghanistan. Gorbachev revealed the truth. Calling the war a 'bleeding wound', the Soviet leader began withdrawing troops. The last Soviet troops left Afghanistan on February 15, 1989. Afghanistan fell into a state of civil war.

Gorbachev's determination to reform Soviet rule began to backfire. His intention was always to retain the USSR. But demands for independence began raising its head – first in the Soviet republics of Azerbaijan and Armenia.

Freedom

Events now moved quickly across Eastern Europe. Demonstrations were erupting in Poland, Hungary, East Germany and elsewhere. The Hungarian government opened its border with its western neighbour, Austria. As a result, thousands of East Germans travelled to Hungary and from there into the West. On August 23, 2 million people held hands and formed a human chain of peace 420 miles long across the three Baltic States. The following day, the first post-war, non-communist eastern European government came to power in Poland, with Solidarity's Tadeusz Mazowiecki becoming the first non-communist Polish prime minister.

In mid-May, in the midst of this turmoil, Gorbachev visited China in an attempt to reconcile the longstanding Sino-Soviet differences. The timing could not have been worse – Chinese students and workers had taken to the streets in Beijing, notably in Tiananmen Square, and several other cities protesting against China's authoritarian rule. There were hunger strikes and violence. The Chinese government imposed martial law. It was only after Gorbachev's departure that the authorities sent in the tanks and crushed the rebellion with extreme force resulting in international condemnation.

On October 7, East Germany held nationwide events to celebrate its 40th year. Gorbachev attended but everywhere he went, he was greeted with calls for freedom. A week later, Erich Honecker, in charge of East Germany since 1971, resigned, to be replaced by Egon Krenz. Krenz immediately promised reform. But it wasn't enough. Demonstrations throughout East Germany (and elsewhere throughout Eastern Europe) gained momentum and confidence. On November 8, with more and more East

Germans escaping into Austria, Krenz dramatically announced that East Berliners could apply for visas to visit West Berlin. Although a massive concession it still was not enough for the crowds already flocking to the Wall. The East German border guards, under enormous pressure, opened the gates. A few East Berliners stepped cautiously through, followed by more. Then, as their confidence grew, people climbed the wall and began hacking at it as the world watched on television. After 28 years, the Berlin Wall, the symbol of the Cold War, had come down.

East Germans hacking at the Berlin Wall, November 1989.

Within days the dreaded East German secret police, the Stasi, was disbanded. In mid-December, the first of 600 border watchtowers was demolished. Within four months

East Germany held its first free election since 1946. As with 45 years earlier, the communists were convincingly beaten. This time however there was no return. Finally on October 3, 1990, after 41 years as a country artificially split into two, East and West Germany were re-united.

Democratic movements moved equally quickly elsewhere. On November 10, the longest-serving Eastern Bloc leader, Todor Zhivkov, Bulgaria's communist leader since 1954, resigned. Non-communist parties re-emerged.

On November 17, in Prague's Wenceslas Square, Czechoslovakian police fired at a protest but over the coming days more and more people came out to demonstrate. The government and police had no answer to this 'Velvet Revolution'. Dubcek, the instigator of the Prague Spring 21 years before, spoke to the crowds, as did the future president, Vaclav Havel, recently released from another spell in prison. Miloš Jakeš, the communist leader, realising that no help would be forthcoming from Moscow, resigned. On December 29, Havel was made president, the last president of Czechoslovakia. Following the dissolution of Czechoslovakia on January 1, 1993, Havel became the first president of the newly-formed Czech Republic.

The fall of the communist states happened peacefully in most of the Eastern Bloc. One exception being

Romania. Nicolae Ceauşescu had been Romania's communist leader since 1965, a regime streaked with corruption. He'd previously rejected Gorbachev's calls for reform. On December 21, 1989, Ceauşescu, sure of his place in his nation's affections, organised a mass gathering in Bucharest's Palace Square in order to rally support. It backfired. His speech was booed. The following day, he tried again. This time the crowd's antagonism held no bounds and together with Elena, his wife *and* deputy prime minister, Ceauşescu made his escape by helicopter. They tried to flee but were caught in the town of Târgovişte. The following day, Christmas Day, the Ceauşescus were tried by a hastily-convened kangaroo court, and promptly executed.

Nicolae Ceausescu and Erich Honecker, November 1988.

The 1990s

The End of the USSR

One by one, the Baltic States (annexed by Stalin in 1940) declared their independence, beginning with Lithuania on March 11, 1990. Gorbachev, still desperate to maintain the union, sent in the tanks. To no avail. On May 4, Latvia also declared its independence followed four days later by Estonia.

The largest of the Soviet states was Russia itself. On May 29, 1990 Boris Yeltsin was elected its chairman. On June 12, 1990, Russia also seceded from the USSR, with Yeltsin now its president. Gorbachev remained in charge of the USSR.

In Hungary on May 2, 1990, Arpad Goncz was elected president by an overwhelming majority, Hungary's first democratically elected head of state and the first non-communist leader in 42 years. Within a month, Hungary had withdrawn from the Warsaw Pact.

Only in Yugoslavia was there widespread and protracted violence. Another artificial country thrown together in 1918, Yugoslavia was made up of several republics. Since the 1980s, regional and ethnic rivalries sprung up which, after the disintegration of the Eastern Bloc, led to a vicious civil war which saw ethnic cleansing and genocide, requiring the intervention of UN forces and NATO.

Gorbachev still believed he could maintain the Soviet Union; its communist party, although severely diminished, was not yet beaten. But the party had lost faith in their leader. In August, while on holiday in the Crimea, the communists interned Gorbachev and told the world's media that he had 'resigned' due to ill-health. Their attempted coup, August 19 – 21, lacked support and was undermined by Yeltsin. Gorbachev returned to Moscow, his position intact. In the midst of this, Armenia, Ukraine and Byelorussia declared their independence, the first non-Baltic republics to secede from the Soviet Union. (Byelorussia subsequently renaming itself Belarus). Other states followed.

Boris Yeltsin speaking outside the Moscow White House, August 19, 1991.

On December 8, the Russian Federation, Belarus and Ukraine formed the Commonwealth of Independent States (CIS). By the end of the month, all the former Soviet republics except the three Baltic States and Georgia had also joined (although Georgia would join two years later). Humiliated by Yeltsin on national television, Gorbachev's position had become untenable. On December 25, 1991, Gorbachev resigned as leader of the Soviet Union. The following day, the Union of Soviet Socialist Republics was officially dissolved.

The Soviet Union, officially founded in 1922, was no more. The 'People's Republics' throughout Eastern Europe were now simply 'Republics'; Germany was one;

secret police forces disbanded, press censorship abolished. People were free to speak and free to write as they wished; they were free to travel and free to worship; they could freely demonstrate, criticize and vote. Finally, after 45 years of totalitarianism, democracy had prevailed. The Cold War was at an end.

The Cold War Timeline

1940s

May 8, 1945	World War Two: Germany surrenders
August 14, 1945	World War Two: Japan surrenders
March 5, 1946	Winston Churchill's 'Iron Curtain' speech.
March 3, 1947	Harry S. Truman proposes the 'Truman Doctrine'.
June 5, 1947	Announcement of the Marshall Plan
February 25, 1948	Communist takeover in Czechoslovakia
June 24, 1948	Start of the Berlin Blockade
April 4, 1949	NATO established
May 12, 1949	End of the Berlin Blockade
May 23, 1949	Formal division between East and West Germany

August 29, 1949	USSR detonate their first atomic bomb
October 1, 1949	People's Republic of China founded

1950s

February 1950	Start of the McCarthy era
June 25, 1950	Start of the Korean War
October 19, 1950	China enters Korean War
November 1, 1952	USA detonate world's first hydrogen bomb
March 3, 1953	Death of Stalin
June 16, 1953	Uprising in East Germany
July 27, 1953	End of Korean War
July 21, 1954	Vietnam divided at the 17th parallel
May 14, 1955	Formation of the Warsaw Pact
February 25, 1956	Khrushchev denounces Stalin's method of rule
June 1956	Polish Uprising
October 23, 1956	Start of Hungarian Uprising
November 1956	Suez Crisis
Nov 10, 1956	End of the Hungarian Uprising
October 4, 1957	Soviet Union launched the first satellite, or Sputnik, into space
January 1958	Chairman Mao launches the Great Leap Forward

January 1, 1959	Fidel Castro takes power in Cuba
September 1959	Khrushchev visits USA
Sept 26, 1959	Start of Vietnam War

1960s

May 1960	US U-2 spyplane shot down over Moscow
April 12, 1961	Soviet astronaut, Yuri Gagarin, becomes the first man in space
April 17, 1961	US-backed Bay of Pigs invasion
August 12-13, 1961	Berlin Wall erected
October 1962	Cuban Missile Crisis
June 1963	John F. Kennedy visits West Berlin
Nov 22, 1963	Assassination of Kennedy
May 16, 1966	Chairman Mao launches the Cultural Revolution
June 5-10, 1967	Arab-Israeli Six-Day War
August 1968	Soviet tanks crush Czechoslovakian revolt
July 20, 1969	USA lands first man on the moon

1970s

February 1972	Richard Nixon visits China
January 15, 1973	Ceasefire between US and North Vietnam

April 30, 1973	South Vietnam accepts defeat
October 1973	Arab-Israeli 'Yom Kippur' war
August 8, 1974	Nixon resigns following Watergate scandal
April 30, 1975	End of Vietnam War
October 1978	Karol Wojtyla appointed Pope John Paul II
January 1979	Islamic republic established in Iran

1980s

Dec 25, 1980	Soviet Union's invasion of Afghanistan
Dec 13, 1981	Martial law imposed in Poland and Solidarity banned
September 1, 1983	Soviet fighter plane shoots down a Korean civilian airliner
June 12, 1987	Ronald Reagan visits West Berlin
January 1989	Soviet troops withdraw from Afghanistan
June 1989	Student uprising in Beijing
August 24, 1989	Poland votes in first non-communist government in post-war Eastern Europe
October 7, 1989	East Germany celebrates fortieth anniversary

November 9, 1989 Fall of the Berlin Wall

Nov 17, 1989 Start of the Velvet Revolution in Czechoslovakia

Dec 25, 1989 Execution of Nicolae and Elena Ceausescu in Romania

1990s

March-May 1990 Baltic States declare independence

October 3, 1990 Germany re-unified

June 12, 1991 Boris Yeltsin elected president of the Russian Federation

June 17, 1991 Warsaw Pact dissolved

June 1991 Last Soviet tanks leave Eastern Europe

August 19, 1991 Communist coup in Russia

December 8, 1991 Founding of the Commonwealth of Independent States

Dec 25, 1991 Mikhail Gorbachev resigns

Images

All the images used in this book are, as far as the publisher can ascertain, in the public domain. If they have mistakenly used an image that is not in the public domain, please let them know at felix@historyinanhour.com and they shall remove / replace the offending item.

Made in the USA
Middletown, DE
12 December 2019